MESA VERDE
National Park

by Ruth Radlauer

Design and photographs
by Rolf Zillmer

AN ELK GROVE BOOK

 CHILDRENS PRESS, CHICAGO

Both author and photographer are
indebted to Gilbert Wenger,
Chief Park Archeologist,
Mesa Verde National Park,
for his help with illustrations
and authentication of the manuscript.

Photo page 35 by Ed Radlauer

Library of Congress Cataloging in Publication Data
Radlauer, Ruth Shaw.
    Mesa Verde National Park.
    ''An Elk Grove book.''
    SUMMARY: Discusses the cliff dwellings found in Mesa
Verde National Park which are believed to have been built
by relatives of the Pueblo Indians.
    1. Pueblo Indians—Antiquities—Juvenile literature.
2. Mesa Verde National Park—Juvenile literature.
3. Colorado—Antiquities—Juvenile literature.
[1. Mesa Verde National Park. 2. Cliff dwellers—
Colorado. 3. Cliff dwellings—Colorado. 4. Pueblo
Indians—Antiquities. 5. Indians of North America—
Antiquities] I. Zillmer, Rolf. II. Title.
E99.P9R16 1977   978.8   76-27350
ISBN 0-516-07490-3

1 2 3 4 5 6 7 8 9 10 11 12 13 14 15 R 82 81 80 79 78 77

Contents

The Mystery of Mesa Verde

Imagine that you, your family, and your neighbors disappeared last Tuesday. When you disappeared, you took nothing with you. How did your room look? What would people find in the trash can behind your house? Could anyone solve the mystery of why you went away?

There's a place in Colorado where whole villages of people disappeared. It seems that about 650 years ago they just walked away and left most of their belongings. Hundreds of years later other people found the belongings and deserted homes. The ruined homes were in big natural caves among Southern Colorado cliffs.

Why did the ancient ones build stone houses in caves? What did they do with the feathered sticks they left there? Who wove the cotton blankets? How did they paint designs on the house walls? And why did they leave?

These are the questions and mysteries of Mesa Verde. May be you can find some of the answers when you visit this National Park.

Mesa Verde—Green Table

Balcony House

Who Lived At Cliff Palace?

How Did They Paint Designs?

Green Table Land

When Spanish explorers first saw the flat-topped mountains in southwest Colorado, they called them "mesas," the Spanish word for "tables." Because the mountains were covered with trees and shrubs, they called the area "green table land," or Mesa Verde. The Spanish didn't get close enough to see the stone houses. They just rode by, looking for a route to California.

Mesa Verde kept its secret until 1874 when W. H. Jackson took a picture of Two Story Cliff House. In 1888 two ranchers, Richard Wetherill and Charles Mason, found their way to the ruins of Cliff Palace.

Now you can find these stone houses by going to Mancos or Cortez, Colorado on Highway 160. The park's entrance is about ten miles from each of these towns. Beyond the entrance the road climbs to the Morfield Campground where you may wish to camp. Ten miles further is the Far View Visitor Center where a Park Ranger can help you plan your stay. Then you can begin collecting the clues you need to understand the mystery of Mesa Verde National Park.

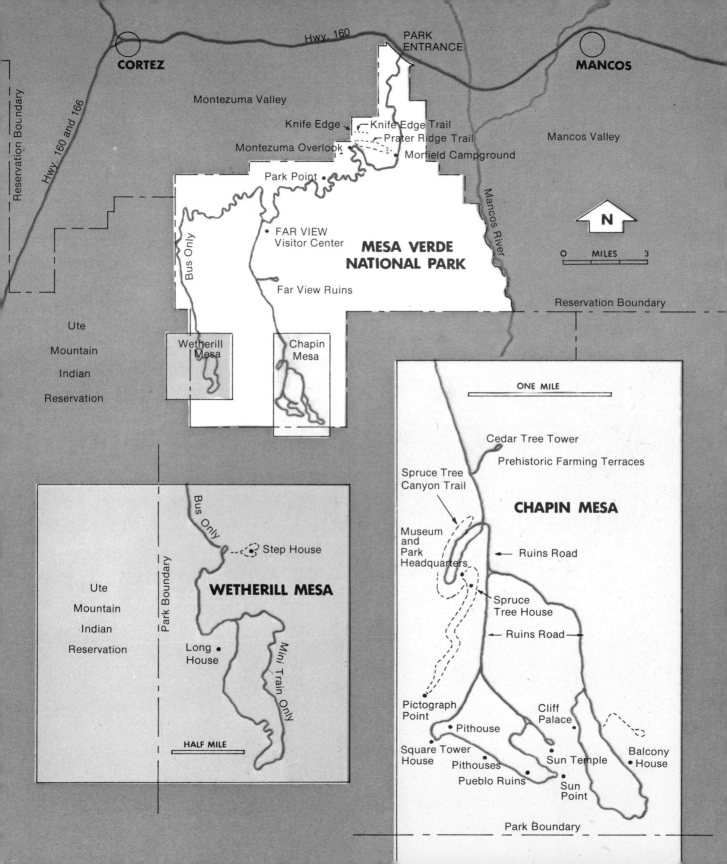

Detectives— Archeologists

Many detectives have worked on the mystery of Mesa Verde for a long time. Some of the detectives are scientists called archeologists. They dig carefully around Mesa Verde to find ruins of houses and artifacts, things people have made.

They find broken clay pots and try to put them together. The designs on the pots and house walls tell the archeologists that the ancient people liked to decorate their belongings.

Sometimes archeologists find skeletons and dried bodies, or mummies. By studying the bodies, other scientists can tell how big the people were and how they lived. Their bones tell us what diseases they had. Teeth in the jawbones show what kind of food they ate. A careful look at the skulls shows that something made the backs of the people's heads flat.

Other detective-scientists use instruments to tell how long ago the bodies were alive and how old the clay pots are. This tells us how long ago people lived at Mesa Verde.

Tools Of The Archeologist

They Try To Put Broken Pots Together

And More Detectives

Other detective-scientists have different tools to tell how old things are. By studying the growth rings of very old trees, they can tell what the weather was like hundreds of years ago. They can also compare the rings of wooden poles found in the houses and tell how old the poles are.

They know that in the year 1268 it rained enough to grow a good crop of corn, beans, and squash. That spring the streams ran full of water. The women could store it in clay jugs to be used in the dry summer months.

The tree-ring calendar shows that 24 years of drought, or dry weather, began a few years later. The people had lived through droughts before. But this time, for some reason, they left. Why? Were they afraid? Did they think witches, or evil spirits wanted them to go away?

Perhaps if you know more about the people and how they lived, you can answer some of these questions.

Ceiling—Modified Basketmaker House

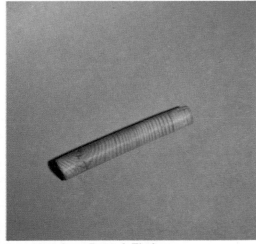

Tree Ring Core From A Timber

Timbers Hold The Balcony—Balcony House

Anasazi— The Old Ones

The Mesa Verde houses built many years ago are much like those built by modern Pueblo Indians. For that reason scientists believe the modern Pueblos are related to the ancient people. By studying modern Pueblo customs, scientists called ethnologists can guess how the ancient ones lived.

Ethnologists can learn how crops may have been planted. They can guess what the children did, who wove the blankets, and who made the bowls found in Mesa Verde ruins.

We don't know what the ancient people called themselves. Modern people have borrowed a Navajo word, "Anasazi," the "old ones," to describe them.

To study the people of Mesa Verde, scientists have divided Anasazi history into four parts.

1. Basketmaker Period	A.D. 1 to 550
2. Modified Basketmaker Period	A.D. 550 to 750
3. Developmental Pueblo Period	A.D. 750 to 1100
4. Great Pueblo Period	A.D. 1100 to 1300

Spruce Tree House ►

Two Periods of Time

In the Basketmaker Period, before the Anasazi came to Mesa Verde, they roamed from place to place. They lived in valleys and caves. This period began about 2000 years ago and lasted until about A.D. 550.

The people wove yucca fibers into baskets, belts, and mats. To keep warm they made robes of furry animal skins. Tools were made of wood, bone, and stone. With dart-throwing tools called atlatls, they hunted deer, elk, and mountain sheep. Near the end of this time they learned to farm.

During the next 200 years the Anasazi found the rich land of Mesa Verde. It was the Modified Basketmaker Period when they learned to make clay pots. With pottery they could cook foods better, so beans were added to the crops they farmed. They kept turkeys and made warm robes from their feathers.

The Anasazi built pit houses in caves and on the mesa tops. The houses were pits, or holes, in the ground. Above the ground were low walls and flat roofs of mud-covered poles and sticks.

At First They Roamed And Hunted— Museum Diorama

They Wove Baskets

Clay Cooking Pot—Modified Basketmaker

Two More Periods

The next period of 350 years was the Developmental Pueblo Period. In that time the Anasazi built their houses close together in small villages, later called pueblos by the Spanish. No longer using pits, the people made houses out of sandstone blocks. The houses stood in a line or curved row around an open space, or court.

In the court was a deep pit lined with stone blocks. This was a ceremonial room called a kiva. From this time on, most houses or groups of houses had kivas.

This was a time of change when trade with tribes to the south brought cotton, shells, and turquoise.

The Great Pueblo Period lasted about 200 years. Houses were closer together in units something like apartment buildings.

During the second half of this period the Anasazi moved their homes to the caves of the canyon walls. Here they built thick, stone-walled houses, kivas, and towers.

Houses Stood In A Curved Row—Developmental Period—Museum Diorama

Kiva—Oak Tree House

Long House

The Mesas—
Chapin
and
Wetherill

Life in the cliff houses was good until something happened to make the Anasazi leave. What did happen? Perhaps you can find some clues.

There are about 12 mesas in the park. But most of the activity goes on around two of them—Chapin and Wetherill.

Chapin Mesa has the Park Museum, Headquarters, and Post Office. By bus, car, or on a bicycle, you can tour Ruins Road to explore the mesa-top ruins. You can also look across canyons at the ruins of later cliff houses. Spruce Tree House, Cliff Palace, and Balcony House are the ones reached from Chapin Mesa. To go to Balcony House, you need a free ticket. You can get your ticket at Far View Visitor Center on your way to Chapin Mesa.

Cars are not allowed at Wetherill Mesa, so buses leave Far View Visitor Center every half hour to take you there. Once at Wetherill, you can walk or take a mini-train to the cliff ruins. Pamphlets help you take self-guided tours of Long House and Step House. You can ask questions of the Ranger on duty.

A Thirty-Foot Ladder Leads To Balcony House

Mini-Train—Wetherill Mesa

Ruins Road

Some mesa-top ruins were found by the people who discovered the cliff houses in 1888. But archeologists hunted for more. They looked for clues such as big, healthy juniper trees and big mounds.

A big juniper tree sometimes led to a pit house because rain and wind filled the pit with dirt after the Anasazi left. The mud and clay lining of a pit house became something like a flower pot, holding water and soil. Any tree that grew in a pit house for many years got bigger than others of the same age.

Archeologists also knew that after hundreds of years, a pueblo was buried by soil, plants, and trees. So they looked for mounds on the flat mesa tops and began to dig carefully.

Ruins Road on Chapin Mesa takes you to all the places, or sites, the archeologists have dug out. Beginning at site one, you see the earliest pit house as the archeologists found it. Nearby you can read about different parts of this one-room house and see paintings of how it might have looked in A.D. 550.

Model of Basketmaker House

Modified Basketmaker House—Ruins Road

View Points

Farther along Ruins Road you find later houses and pictures of how they looked when people lived in them.

Little by little the people made better houses. By A.D. 1100 they chipped and shaped stones to make blocks. With mud they cemented the stones together to make walls. But then the people began to take some of the stones away to the overhangs or caves in the cliffs. Here again they built houses of stone blocks cemented together with mud. To make all that mud, they had to carry water up from the valley. So they saved water by filling some of the space between stones with small rocks.

On Ruins Road are many view points where you can look across and see ruins of these homes. Again you wonder why. The more you look, the more questions you have to ask.

Were the people giants? Is that how they could build such high towers? But if they were giants, how could they get into the houses through those tiny doors?

See Sun Temple From Sun Point

You Can Climb On Sun Temple

They Put Rocks In The Mud Between Blocks

Kivas And Towers—Cliff Palace

Cliff Houses

Cliff houses were built and used during the last 100 years the Anasazi spent at Mesa Verde, from about A.D. 1200 to 1300.

In summer you can see Cliff Palace, Spruce Tree House, and Wetherill cliff houses on self-guided tours when Park Rangers are on duty. The Rangers answer questions and make sure the ruins, as well as the visitors, are safe.

At Spruce Tree House you can see how a kiva looks with a roof on it. You can climb down a ladder into the kiva and see how the roof was made. Ask the Ranger at Cliff Palace to show you where the wall paintings are.

Step House ruin in a cave at Wetherill Mesa has a Modified Basketmaker pit house. It stands beside a bigger house built about 500 years later. The Park Service rebuilt this pit house to show how it was built with poles, sticks, and mud. The flat roof has a hole in the center where people went in and out. This ruin is called Step House because the Anasazi built stone steps down into the cave.

Spruce Tree House Kivas Have Roofs

Climb Down Into A Kiva

Modified Basketmaker House—Step House Ruin

Spring
A.D. 1265

The studies of ethnologists help us imagine how it might have been to live here in the Great Pueblo Period. For women, spring was a busy time after the long cold winter. They cleaned walls and painted new designs on them. They made new bowls and pots. Men and boys waited for planting time.

Spring was also a time for marriages. If a girl was to marry she had to squat in front of the boy's house and grind corn for four days. If her grinding was good, the families agreed on the marriage.

The boy began working to make gifts for his bride. He might weave yucca fiber sandals or a cotton blanket for her. While he was busy making gifts, the girl's family built a house for the young couple.

When the day finally came, the young man moved his belongings into the new house. If the marriage went well, they had children and lived to the "old" age of about 35.

If the man wanted to end the marriage he took his belongings and left. If the wife wanted to end the marriage, she put her husband's belongings outside while he was away.

In Spring They Made New Pottery

The Boy Wove Sandals Of Yucca Fibers

Spring Planting

The village sun watcher knew by the sunrise and sunset when it was time to plant. If farmers planted too soon, the corn might freeze in the ground. Too late, their crops would have no rain for sprouting. At planting time each man took six different colors of corn seeds to his field on the mesa top.

He used a digging stick to put four holes around a center spot—north, west, south, and east. Then he dug holes at northwest and southeast.

Placing a feathered prayer stick in the center, he knelt and chanted as he dropped four yellow seeds in the north hole. Facing west, he put four blue seeds in that hole, red in the south, and white in the east. Speckled corn went into the northwest hole, while black corn went into the southeast one.

With each hole covered, the farmer planted four rows of corn. These went out from the center to north, west, south, and east. Then, after four days of prayer, he returned to plant the rest of the field.

The Sun Watcher Knew

FARMING IMPLEMENTS

DIGGING OR PLANTING STICKS

DIGGING STICK WITH STONE BLADE

Farming Tools

Summer

Then, as now, summer was dry. Corn had been planted deep enough to reach the snow that had melted into the ground. Early each day, the farmers ran to the mesa tops to chop the weeds that might rob their crops of water.

During the heat of the day, men sat in the shade and chipped stone tools and whittled bows.

Day and night boys watched the crops to keep the ravens, rabbits, and squirrels away. At night they kept the witches away by smearing ashes on their faces.

At home women made many trips to the springs below the cliffs where water seeped through sandstone. With ladles, or big spoons, they dipped water into clay jars. Then they balanced the heavy jars on their heads and carried them up the cliffs and ladders to their houses.

Women also gathered wild plants for food and medicine—wild onions, prickly pears, lily bulbs, the flower and stem of yucca, and many other plants. These added flavor to their meals or took away toothaches and colds.

Man-Made Stone Tools

A Ring Of Woven Yucca Protected The Head From A Heavy Water Jar

Fall

Laughing, happy voices must have echoed around the canyons of Mesa Verde when fall turned the leaves to gold and brown. Hard work had produced many ears of corn and other foods for the long winter ahead.

Fires glowed in the fields at night while men and boys kept the deer from nibbling at the harvest. During the day ravens and crows had to be chased away from the heavy ears of corn.

Soon everyone joined to pick beans, squash, and corn. They beat the dried beans to free them from their pods, then carried the harvest to the cliffs.

Each roof and courtyard and every cliff city became a mass of color as food was spread to dry.

High above the houses, in cracks of cave walls were the storage rooms. Jars of beans and stacks of corn and dried squash soon filled them.

As November days brought a dusting of snow, people must have smiled as they looked at the full storage rooms. They were ready to face the long, cold winter.

They Chased Deer From The Crops

Stacks Of Corn Filled The Storage Rooms

Winter

In winter the snow and zero temperatures made Mesa Verde life hard. To keep warm, people huddled inside a smoky house by a fire or stood over an outdoor fire in the courtyard.

When a boy became a man, he could spend some of the winter in a warm kiva. The kiva was a sort of clubhouse for men and a place for ceremonies.

The round kiva had no windows. A hole in the roof let out smoke from the fire. A ladder leaned against the hole for people to climb in and out.

Air came down into the kiva through a small ventilator, something like a chimney. As air entered the kiva, it hit a low wall, the deflector, and flowed around the room.

Most kivas had benches (banquettes) built into the walls. A small pit near the center held the fire. Every kiva had a smaller hole near the firepit, the sipapu (see-pa-poo). The sipapu was a symbol of the place from which all living things came up out of "mother earth."

The Museum

The story of life at Mesa Verde is shown by artifacts, bones, models, and dioramas in the Park Museum near Spruce Tree House.

Many artifacts were taken away from Mesa Verde before it became a national park in 1906. Ever since then, artifacts have been protected just as animals are protected in national parks.

If you find an artifact such as a piece of broken pottery, called a sherd, give it to a Ranger. It may end up in the museum where it will be seen by millions of people.

The mysterious story of the Anasazi unfolds in the museum displays. Turkey feather robes, yucca fiber sandals, and sashes made of dog hair hang in cases to show Anasazi clothing.

Digging sticks, ancient beans, and 700-year-old ears of corn tell us how people farmed to feed themselves.

You can even see human backbones and leg bones. Skulls, flattened at the back, show that mothers used unpadded cradle boards to carry their babies.

Take time to read about each display in this amazing museum.

Sherds

Skulls Were Flattened At The Back

Your Trip To Mesa Verde

National parks may be crowded in summer, especially on holidays and weekends. Some say it's best to go to Mesa Verde in mid-June and early fall.

It may take you two or three days to see all you want. It takes two or three hours to tour all of Ruins Road. Many people drive the loops twice, at different times of day. You could spend at least half a day in the Park Museum.

In planning your trip, add enough time to do all the other things you like. You might hike, ride a horse, or hunt wildlife with a camera.

What you take along depends on what you like to do. Climbing around the ruins is more fun in strong, comfortable hiking shoes or boots. A sun hat, longsleeved shirt, and canteen will be good on long, hot hikes. If you have binoculars, you'll enjoy using them. Your pet will be happier at home, but your bicycle may come in handy on Ruins Road or at Morfield Campground.

Hunt Wildlife With A Camera— Collared Lizard

Pictograph Point

Many ancient people have tried to "write" in pictures. If people painted pictures on stone, we call them *pictographs.* If the pictures are pecked, or scratched, into the stone, they're called *petroglyphs.*

On a hike to Pictograph Point, you will see some petroglyphs. The point was named in the 1930s before someone had learned the difference between pictographs and petroglyphs.

The hike from the canyon near Spruce Tree House to the Point and back to the museum takes about two hours. The trail goes along the side of Spruce Tree Canyon where you'll see caves, trees, bushes, and sometimes wildflowers. The view of other mesas gets better as you climb the trail. When the trail gets steep, look up at the rocks above your head. Soon you'll see the petroglyphs pecked in the rock hundreds of years ago.

Some modern Hopi Indians tried to read the petroglyphs. The Hopi Indians said the petroglyphs told about the Anasazi's early travels. The story tells how different family groups, or clans, stopped here and there to make their homes.

Pictographs are Painted

Petroglyphs Are Pecked Out Of Rock

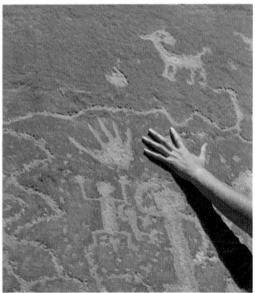

Whose Hands Pecked These?

Other Hikes

There are still many ruins in Mesa Verde National Park that have not been dug up. That's why hiking is carefully controlled in this park.

When you go to Pictograph Point or hike Spruce Tree Canyon Trail, you sign a card at the beginning of the trail. Leave part of the card in the box and carry the other part with you. Turn in the part you carried at the Museum so the Rangers will know you got back OK.

Two trails near Morfield Campground are open to all hikers without permits. Prater Ridge Trail begins near the stables, loops up over the ridge of a mesa, and back to the campground. The hike takes about six hours unless you take a marked shortcut, making the hike only three hours. On a one-hour hike to Knife Edge and back, you'll see all of Montezuma Valley.

If you like "hiking on two wheels," you can rent a bicycle at Spruce Tree Store every day in the summer. Bicycles are allowed only on Chapin Mesa. Here you can pedal two loops on Ruins Road.

Knife Edge

From Knife Edge You can See Montezuma Valley

Why?

How many mysteries will you solve before you leave Mesa Verde National Park? One mystery is why the Anasazi decided to leave the mesa tops and build villages in the overhangs of cliffs. Old people could not go in and out very easily, and young children could fall into the canyon. Men and boys had to run to the mesa-top fields every day from planting time until after harvest.

An even bigger mystery is why the people left these homes after they worked so hard to build them. Long years of dry weather caused small groups to leave. The Anasazi had suffered droughts before. Perhaps this drought lasted too long.

Maybe attacking enemies or sickness forced them to leave. Maybe the soil could no longer produce good crops. Had they used up all the trees for building?

Finally, they all left. Where did they go? Clues point south to New Mexico and Arizona. No one really knows for sure. There will always be mysteries at Mesa Verde National Park.

The Mysteries Remain At Square Tower House ▶

Another Park in Colorado

In ROCKY MOUNTAIN NATIONAL PARK there are good roads and 200 miles of hiking trails. They take you to sparkling lakes, rushing streams, and beaver ponds.

At this park a person can drive up Trail Ridge Road past snowy peaks to the tundra. Tundra means a land of no trees. The cold icy wind that whips across the tundra makes plant growth difficult. Plants that do grow here are tiny and hug the ground.

A backpacker's delight, Rocky Mountain National Park also offers many other interesting activities: history and nature walks, beaver walks, evening programs, and half-day and all-day guided hikes.

Here is truly another PARK FOR PEOPLE.

Sheep Lake—Rocky Mountain National Park ▶

The Author and Illustrator

Wyoming-born Ruth Radlauer's love affair with National Parks began in Yellowstone. During her younger years she spent her summers in the Bighorn Mountains, in Yellowstone, or in the mountains near Casper.

Ed and Ruth Radlauer, graduates of the University of California at Los Angeles, are authors of many books for young people. Their subjects range from social studies to youth activities such as horse riding and motorcycles.

The Radlauers live in California, where they spend most of their time in the mountains near Los Angeles.

Photographing the national parks is a labor of love for Rolf Zillmer and his wife Evelyn. Because they are backpackers and wildlife enthusiasts, the Zillmers can give a truly intimate view of each park.

A former student at Art Center College of Design in Los Angeles, Mr. Zillmer was born in New York City. He now makes his home in Missoula, Montana, where he does painting, sculpture, and most of the art direction for Elk Grove Books.